In these compact and powerf⸻
breaks through a bitter imprisonmer⸻
like vision, the force of which is adn⸻
adaptation of Sonia Raiziss.

William Jay Smith

— William Jay Smith

De Palchi's outrage at the gruesome war that surrounded and invaded him cruelly in his youth in Italy at the height of the Second World War found its expression in many syntactically tormented poems with which he began to write. It was as though the adumbrated syntax acted as a kind of metaphor for what was inexpressible, except for such signs as in dumb language: a fierce waving of arms and elbows, eyes flaring. From time to time, as de Palchi absorbs the first blows of disbelief, poems emerge fully expressive, charged with their art of anger and sarcasm. Here you have in essence de Palchi's youthful masterwork.

David Ignatow

— David Ignatow

The author (Paris, 1952)

Alfredo de Palchi

The Scorpion's Dark,
Dance,

la buia danza di
scorpione

A Xenos Dual-Language Edition

Translated from the Italian
&
introduced

by

Sonia Raiziss

XENOS BOOKS

Front cover: *Gossip* (1990)
A sculpture of toy guns, pine needles,
cedar twigs and hardware by Jerilea Zempel
Reproduced with permission of the artist

Back cover: *Alfredo de Palchi* (1970)
A drawing by Rose Graubart Ignatow
Reproduced with permission of the artist

Library of Congress Cataloging-in-Publication Data

De Palchi, Alfredo, 1926-
    [Principium. English & Italian]
    La buia danza di scorpione = The scorpion's dark dance / Alfredo
de Palchi; translated from the Italian and introduced by Sonia
Raiziss
        p.   cm.
    English and Italian
    "A Xenos dual-language edition."
    ISBN 1-879378-06-X (cloth) : $19.95 -- ISBN 1-879378-05-1 (paper)
: $9.95
    1. De Palchi, Alfredo, 1926- --Translations into English.
I. Raiziss, Sonia. II. Title. III. Title: Scorpion's dark dance.
PQ4864.E6P7513   1993
851'.914--dc20   93-16133
                                                                    CIP

Designed by Karl Kvitko. Published by Xenos Books, P.O. Box 52152,
Riverside, CA. 92517-3152.   Printed in the United States of America by
Van Volumes Ltd., Thorndike, MA. 01079

TABLE OF CONTENTS

La Buia Danza di Scorpione / *The Scorpion's Dark Dance*

III. CARNEVALE D'ESILIO

III. A CARNIVAL OF EXILES

vii

The Poetic Sting

With Alfredo de Palchi the poet is the man. What he has known, what he has lived, is what he writes. He's one of the most instinctive, shall I say "natural," poets I know. His feelings become his words, his words originate from what life has dealt him; they swirl, leap and sing from the fire within — born of sharp stings and shooting spontaneously through his flesh.

So his concern is not how to dress the wounds in appropriate words and present them poetically. The poet is the sufferer, and the experience is the metaphor closest to itself. This is what happened, this is how it was.

And as he cries out for himself and for all those who were intimates of his early life, he takes little interest in mere adjectives, adverbs, images for themselves. The initial experience, the feelings that explode in hot geysers from the source — these become the poem. It is this deep hurt, mixed with his blood, that eventually declares itself in a knotted, rough scar of tense words.

Style makes the man, according to the adage. But in de Palchi's case the formula is reversed. He is altogether himself. If his language is direct, unadorned, unconcerned with flow, figuration, fancy, it is not because he aims to match a style, but rather because the fact, the act, is its own nearest and truest protest. And because the experience is so internal, the reader must guess how far down it goes; the extraction of meaning becomes difficult for both translator and reader.

Thus it is with a true original. He seldom, if ever, has a public or even private agenda of rebellion. Hearing the cries of pain at the twists of life's tourniquets, he recognizes them as his own. The revolt that swells up in his throat does not blend in with a chorus. He joins no school of political thought or artistic form. He follows no stereotypes or modish slants. He has no mentor, though he may keep certain poets close to his heart — in this case, Villon, Rimbaud...

All this accounts for the ineluctable spare effect of his imagery: hard, jagged, spasmodic. His poetic explosions are not always easy to apprehend, but there is a power that transcends conventional expression. The word/sound in them is so basic that it can only be described as unique to this poet. Here is an avant-gardist who preceded his era and leaps ahead into a nameless mood and expletive: himself.

De Palchi's poems are staccato bits of agony spitting out of his guts. No wonder he has so little regard for the look or tune of them. His words are instigated by the pure push of an underground, undersea gush, rising to a shout or curse and then collapsing, often abruptly. No care here for ornament, artifice, euphony. The sounds and symbols in the poems come directly from the poet's experience of the world, the facts of his subterranean existence. The syntax is dictated by his five senses. It is not elaborated for the sake of sentiment or sensation; there is only enough for the sense.

The Scorpion's Dark Dance is primal and not pretty. It emerged from the wrenching of body and soul that de Palchi endured for several years in political incarceration. For both man and poet they were unforgettable and unforgivable years. And the sting is still sharp.

Sonia Raiziss

Sonia Raiziss
New York, 1993

Letter from a Fellow Poet

February 15, 1993

Dear Alfredo de Palchi:

Thank you for allowing me the privilege of reading your fine poems in such strongly imagistic, rhythmical English. These poems are, in your own words, "fragmentary, sometimes incoherent outbursts" of horror and recognition, and in their powerful imagery, their touches of surrealism and relentless probing into the nightmare vision of World War II (any war), they greatly remind me of Lorca's and Radnoti's powerful poems on the same theme. And throughout the rise and fall, the "staccato bits of agony," you have created a speaker who is so fully human and vulnerable and yet defiant, I have to acknowledge my fellow humanity with him/her at every word. I love, for instance, the painful truth of the ever-recurring visitation of nightmare in such a scene as —

> To hear
> no more the thump of the bullet-riddled in the wheat
> the shrieks of the old mouths, the beasts
> trapped by fire and the dark sloshing
> in the Adige...

But I love even more the fact that you soon follow such a vision with these lines of the human spirit forever rebuilding amongst the ruins:

> Already the mason in the yard is rebuillding the house
> brick by brick

You do not ornament the horror with extravagant claims or phrasings, but honestly represent it with clear statement and strong images — which, indeed, makes the devastation so crystalline the reader cannot leave it behind when he stops reading. Who can forget such images as —

> The mother's knuckles beat at the door
> a bridge answers with upended steel roots —
> and who's the one passing
> along the embankments of defeat overturning cages of
> barbed wire

Or —

> A memory of cornstalks cracked by the slaughtered
> still in flight

Such precise, unadorned poetic phrasings rank with the best of Lorca's and Radnoti's poems, and they have the same strengths of personal, original poetic statement that many of the contemporary Eastern European poets presently being translated have. We are in your debt for creating such fine poems from such apocalyptic experiences: the fires have made the poems that much stronger and finer. Especially with a speaker who, although he clearly sees "the bullies have the last word," still tries not to "succumb to the rough rages of hate" and ends with a final "no/no/no."

Thank you for writing these strong, committed poems. I hope they receive the wide audience they deserve.

Very sincerely yours,

Len Roberts

Letter from a Fellow Poet

Many of the English versions of these poems were
first published in the following journals:

The American Poetry Review
Blue Unicorn
Croton Review
The Falcon
Gradiva
Granite
The Hampden-Sydney Poetry Review
International Poetry Review
New Letters
Occum Ridge Review
Paintbrush
Poetry Now
Small Moon
Vortex — A Critical Review

First Italian publications:

"Con piedi cercatori" in *Almanacco dello Specchio* Nº 11
"Mi dicono di origini," "Al palo del telegrafo orrechio il ronzio,"
"In mano ho il seme," "S'abbatte il pugno," "Una scatola"
in *Mutazioni*

A. (signature)

The Scorpion's Dark Dance

Ce monde n'est qu'abusion

François Villon

I. IL PRINCIPIO

I. THE FIRST CAUSE

Il principio

innesta l'aorta nebulosa

e precipita la coscienza

con l'abbietta goccia che spacca

l'ovum

originando un ventre congruo

d'afflizioni

The first cause

engrafts the nebulous aorta

and quickens consciousness

with the abject drop that splits

the egg

starting the womb

fit for affliction

5

Mi dicono di origini
sgomente in queste acque: qui sono erede
figlio limpido — ed amo il fiume
inevitabile
in cui l'intrigo del mio tempo
si accomoda

osservo nel fondo rotolare l'isola
verso il nulla
         l'età muta calore
         il vespaio del gorgo
e l'uno vuole il perché dell'altro:
tu sempre uguale, io
dissennato

They tell me of my dismayed
origins in these waters: here I am the heir
the limpid son — and I love the
ineluctable
river where the intrigues of my time
adjust

deep down I observe my island roll
toward nothingness
              the age has changed its ardor
              the eddy its hornet's nest
and each wants the why of the other:
you ever the same, I
going mad

Al palo del telegrafo orecchio il ronzio

il sortire incandescente da quando

le origini estreme

provocano la terra

                percepisco

accensioni e dovunque mi sparga

chiasso d'inizio odo

My ear at the telegraph pole I catch the hum

the incandescent emergence since the time

when earliest origins

provoke the earth

                        I perceive

sparks igniting and wherever I'm scattered

I hear the uproar of beginnings

In mano ho il seme

nero di girasole —

so che la luce cala dietro

l'inconscio / ma altre nebule

avanzano

        e ho questo seme

da trapiantare

come unico dei sistemi

sconosciuti

I hold a black

sunflower seed in my hand —

knowing that the light sinks behind

the unconscious / but other nebulae etc.

are advancing

               and I have this seed

to transplant as if

unique in the un-

known systems

Primavera

   è una colomba

che pilucca i semi della noia e urta

la soglia

    — mai mi abbandono

alla sua ingordigia o mi abituo

alla vanità ma

la volubilità che m'incanta allunga

il becco sui semi della noia

Spring

      is a pigeon pecking at

seeds of tedium and hustles

at my doorsill

            — never will I

abandon myself to its greed nor get used to

such folly

but the fickleness that charms me stretches its

beak toward the seed of boredom

Nel chiasso

di germogli ed uccelle

la porta spalanca la corsa

in gara col baccano del gallo

sotto la tettoia di zinco

e m'incontra l'argine con l'officina

trebbie e cortili che alzano un fumo

buono di letame

— la pista mi svela

lo scompiglio e odo

un punta di luce scalfirmi gli occhi

In the fluster

of shoots and birds

the door thrusts open to the contest

of the rooster's racket

under the tin roof

and the riverbank meets me with machineshops

threshing floors barnyards that raise a ripe

smoke of manure

                — the pathway reveals

this commotion to me and I hear

a point of light scratching my eyes

Estate

frutto propizio   seno biondo

d'una calata di sensazioni

nel belato d'alberi la luce astringente

urta

tutto scompiglia: il verde-

verde

il cielo-cielo e il rombo . . .

Summer

propitious fruit   blond breast

heavy with an onrush of sensations

in the bleating of trees the astringent light

collides

upsets it all: the green-

green

the sky-sky and the rumble . . .

Ciminiere   fabbriche

del concime e dello zucchero

barconi di ghiaia e qualche gatto

lanciato dal ponte

snaturano questa lastra di fiume

questo Adige

Smokestacks   fertilizer-
works and sugar refineries
barges loaded with gravel and a few cats
flung from the bridge
pervert this slab of river
this Adige

Vortica una fanfara

di zanzare nel crepuscolo

e la giostra del mondo

una fiera di ritagli di luce

— io, incerto

giro il vertiginoso cuore impestato

di zanzare

A fanfare of swirling

mosquitoes in the sunset

and the world's a merry-go-round

a festival of snippets of light

— as for me, wavering

I ride this vertiginous heart plagued

by mosquitoes

Con piedi cercatori
pesanti più che ali d'inverno
vado incontro alla luce

ho gli occhi pesti come
dopo l'incendio terrestre
la notte
la volontà di vedere quello che d'abitudine
si dimentica

Gone searching with a tread
weightier than wings in winter
I shuffle toward the light

      with my eyes bruised
      like the evening
      after the earth's bonfire
      I long to see what we habitually
      forget

Il lepidottero barcolla ai vetri —

mi alzo dai fogli dove sono

insicuro ed apro la finestra

fuore di sé insiste a frenarsi

squama alla luce — io fuori di senno

persisto la buia danza

di scorpione

The moth rocks at the glass panes
I rise from the pages where I feel
uneasy and open the window

beside itself, insistent, it brakes
at the light and flakes off — out of my mind
I persist in doing the scorpion's
dark dance

II. UN'OSSESSIONE DI MOSCHE

II. AN OBSESSION OF FLIES

S'abbate il pugno

sul totale formicolio

della natura — è

sofferenza questo gesto

sulla vorace indifesa

degli insetti e

di me

Down slams the fist

on the total

teeming of nature — this

gesture suffers

over the helpless

voracity of

insects and

my own

Contratto tra convulsioni di case

e agguati

osservo un passaggio di autocarri

e mentre scoppiano argini e barconi

nuoto verso rive ascoltate

— lo sforzo

mi guasta ad ogni bracciata

e i miei pochi anni nuotano con astuzia

di pesci ai fianchi

Caught between convulsions of buildings

and ambush

I observe the cortege of trucks

and while docks explode and the barges

I swim toward the shores heard far off

— the exertion

exhausts me at every stroke

and my few years swim with the cunning

of fish at my side

Ad ogni sputo d'arma scatto

mi riparo dietro l'albero e rido

isterico

alla bocca che sbava

un'ossessione di mosche

At every spit of the gun I jump
I hide back of a tree and laugh
hysterically
seeing that mouth slobber
an obession of flies

Una madre sradicata del ventre geme

per il figlio:

       occhi sbucciati

infiammato groppo di lingua

al palo del telefono penzola con me

afferrato alle gambe

Womb uprooted a mother moans

for her son:

        shelled eyes

swollen knot of a tongue

from the telephone pole he swings with me

clutched to his legs

Dopo l'ultima raffica

il subentrare della calma orrenda

un prete esce pazzo dal fosso

con uno straccio di cristo

impalato

After the last hail of bullets

comes the horrible calm

out of the ditch a priest madly emerges

with a scrap of christ

impaled

Non più
udire il tonfo dei crivellati nel grano
urli di vecchie bocche e di bestie
negli incendi e bui guazzi
nell'Adige

                vedere un branco di vili osservare
chi s'affloscia al muro
il camion che di botto lascia al lampione
chi fa le boccacce con eloquente
groppo di lingua

To hear

no more the thumps of the bullet-riddled in the wheat

the shrieks of old mouths, the beasts

trapped by fire and the dark sloshing

in the Adige

        nor see a pack of cowards

watching a body slump at the wall

the truck suddenly let go at the streetlamp

one who makes faces with his eloquent

lump of a tongue

Al limite del paese le vie

come antenne dilungano

racchiudono il boato e l'angoscia di uomini

che spiandosi in giacche succinte

di precauzione

vilmente si evitano

At the town limits

the streets lengthen like antennae

hold the rumbling and the anguish of men

spying in tight jackets

of precaution

cowards shunning each other

Al richiamo del gallo non evito

la piazza irosa

che inventa leggi — presto

un falso fazzoletto rosso

anche ai miei 18 anni

At the first crowing of the cock

I don't shy from

the angry mob in the square

making its own laws — presto

a fake red scarf

even for me, at 18

Appigliata alle spalle la colomba

annunzia la condanna

odore del diluvio

e l'albero di fuoco

sbracia i rami

strillanti nel cielo basso di fango —

lo spavento dell'uccella difforma

l'innocenza che non si rifugia nell'arca

44

Clinging to their shoulders the dove
utters doom
the smell of the flood,
and the fiery tree
drives branches shrieking into mudslides
from a lowering sky
the bird's terror corrupts an
innocence that finds no shelter in the ark

Già nel cantiere il muratore rimbastisce la casa

con mattone e mattone

all'uscio batte le nocche la madre

risponde con radici d'acciaio rovesciate il ponte

— e chi è che passa

sugli argini della disfatta ribaltando i reticolati

Already the mason in the yard is rebuilding the house
brick by brick

       the mother's knuckles beat at the door

a bridge answers with upended steel roots
— and who's the one passing
along the embankments of defeat overturning cages of
barbed wire

Al calpestio di crocifissi e crocifissi

sputo secoli di vecchie pietre

strade canicolari

il pungente sterco di cavalli immusoniti

in siepi di siccità

(al gomito dell'Adige allora crescevo

di indovinazioni rumori d'altre città)

e sputo sui compagni che mi tradirono

e in me chi forse mi ricorda

At the trampling of crosses upon crosses
I spit out centuries of ancient stones
dogday roads
and the piquant dung of horses sulking
in the hedges of drought

(at the elbow of the Adige I grew up
on guesses, rumors of other cities)

and I spit on the buddies who betrayed me and inside
me on those who may remember

Nel giorno della disfatta cerco la verità

sono il campo vinto
ragazzo armato di ferite

il suolo calpestato
idolo d'argilla

il pane della discordia
la trave nell'occhio

la fionda che punta il mondo
scroscio d'oro del gallo

nel giorno della disfatta trovo la verità

On the day of defeat I search the truth

I am the conquered battlefield
a boy armed with wounds

the trampled soil
idol of clay

bread of discord
the rafter in the eye

the sling that points at the world
golden crash of the rooster

on the day of defeat I find that truth

51

III. CARNEVALE D'ESILIO

III. A CARNIVAL OF EXILES

Dopo una lunga attesa la Rimbaudiana
bellezza mi viene sui ginocchi

le chiedo dell'afflizione e mi offre
la gioia che rifiuto

ancora aspetto
la bruttura che possiede

After a long wait the beauty of Rimbaud

comes to sit on my knees

it's grief I crave but she offers me

joy which I spurn

still expecting

all the bitterness she holds

L'incubo si srotola

sbiscia nel frullare delle piante

dal soffitto

dal muro circolare che imprigiona la luce

essudata d'un olio buio —

non decifro le pagine bibliche

inerti all'occhio che matura

la notte / pelaghi di sonno via

mi portano: margini burroni,

mi muovo lento

la distanza è nera e i passi

sono balzi al rallento mentre le braccia

annaspano ...

The incubus uncoils and

snakes through the ripple of leaves

from the ceiling

from the circular wall that imprisons the bed-

lamp with its sweat of coal oil —

I can't decipher the bible

pages, inert to the eye aging

the night / oceans of sleep drag me

away: borders ravines,

I move heavy

distance hangs black

my steps are leaps in slow motion and my arms

wander ...

Uovo che si lavora nella luce ovale

nuovo adamo

invigorisco nell'altrui simulazione

e quindi anch'io implacabile   finzione

anch'io sono, io

mi credo

altri osserva che non sono —

com'è possibile

se sulla croce di tutti ulcerata

mi svuoto le gote

se circondato non c'è chi

mi disseti

solo chi impreca

Egg laboring in oval light

the new adam

I grow stronger through the feigning of others

and therefore implacable too   a sham

but here I am

believing myself

what others observe I am not —

how can this be

if there on the cankered cross of us all

I gasp with empty cheeks

and crowded around me there's no one to

slake my thirst

only to curse me

Mi condannate

mi spaccate le ossa ma non riuscite

a toccare quello che penso di voi:

gelosi della intelligenza e del neutro

coraggio aggredito dal cono infesto

delle cimici

— io, ricco pasto per voi insetti,

oltre l'ispida luce

vi crollo addosso il pugno

You condemn me
you crack my bones but can't
touch what I think of you:
jealous of my meaning of a neutral
courage attacked by noxious conical
bedbugs

 — me, a rich meal for you insects,
  beyond the bristling light
  I crack my fist down

A boati il vento mi cozza nella cella

dove sono intracciabile —

la mia mano di sepolto

è ugale a quella d'altri che altrove

si tentano uniscono e separano

non lasciando una traccia

qui

l'indifferenza livella tutti

The bellowing wind butts me into the cell

where buried alive I'm not tracked down —

my hand is now like

other hands elsewhere that try to touch, join

but part

without a trace

here

indifference levels us all

Fra le quattro ali di muro

circolo straniero a pugno

serrato — non ho amicizie

non mischio occasionali smanie

con chi le persiste

e siccome ognuno impone

il proprio mondo a chi perde

non si chieda cosa avviene:

la parola è nella bocca dei forti

Between the four wings of walls
a stranger roving with both fists
clenched — I don't make friends
I don't mix my occasional longings
with those who insist on them
and since each one imposes
his own world on a loser
don't ask what happens:
the bullies have the last word

Concluso fra pareti vilipendio

e menzogne

mi sfinisco per quello che succede

mai — non so

non so chi e cosa dovrebbe

capitare: un figlio come me

un quaderno di scritture per testimonianza

un'arma che mi geli

o una migliore conflagrazione

Between walls, abuse and

men's lies I'm finished

I waste myself for something that never

happens — I don't know

                    I don't know who or what

could turn up: a guy like myself

a dossier of entries as evidence

a weapon that freezes me

or some better apocalypse

Il mio tempo tra muri infetti

è un ricordo di spighe rovinato dagli uccisi

ancora in fuga

        — il suolo li sigilla in cedimenti

        di ruggine —

e dall'occhio che indaga laconico.

My time between blighted walls
a memory of cornstalks cracked by the slaughtered
still in flight
           — the ground seals them in sinkholes
           of rust —
and by the laconic eye that probes

Che cogliere dalle disfatte

se tutte le malattie

le vivo — ferro e paglia

m'induriscono la faccia inquadrata

dalle sbarre crescenti

si apra il cancello

la città nella conca schiuma di luci

What can I salvage from defeat

if I still live on all

its ills — iron and straw

harden my features framed by the lengthening bars

open the gate

the city in the hollow foams with lights

Pane è pietra

la sete pietra

ho metri di pietra

mordo la pietra

chiedo acqua

      — mi si impone sete

voglio luce

      mi si impone ombra

calce viva che rosica le mani occupate

a scacciare l'oscurità

la luce è dispensata

quanto l'acqua di cisterna

'vivo! è bello vivere'

mi sorreggo

ma i ghigni intorno mi ghermiscono

Bread is stone

thirst is stone-dry

I walk yards of stone

I bite into stone

I ask for water

            — they inflict thirst

I want light

            — they enforce darkness

quicklime eats into my hands

busy with scattering shadows

light is doled out

like water from a tank

"alive! it's good to live"

that's how I hold up

but sneers all around claw me

Età cruda

fame cruda

una gamella al giorno di ceci col baco

e un pane benzoino

sbadiglio per la fame

mi piego in pena

e vivo di notizie che raccontano quella secca

il suo scheletro nelle baracche

appigliata alle reti elettriche

Raw times
raw hunger
a daily mess tin of chickpeas with worms
and a chunk of benzine bread

I yawn out of hunger
double up in pain
and live on news telling of that gauntness
(its skeleton in the barracks)
hooked on electrified fences

Il pezzo di pane mi nutre

in una putredine di patria

e traffico di truffatori

— il pane

sa di petrolio

lo mastico con bucce di limone

raccolte nelle immondizie

A heel of stale bread feeds me

in the rot of my homeland

an endless traffic of swindlers

— the bread has

a gasoline taste

I chew it with lemon

rinds scrounged from the dump

All'alba morchia — morchia
di caffè con sale
eiaculazioni
c'è chi va e chi viene — si esce al cancello
per indovinare

         'piove?'
non piove
mezzogiorno stagna la monotonia
la puzza del bugliolo
il giornale che tarma
la giornata: consuete notizie

The dregs of dawn — dregs

of coffee salted for sweetness

ejaculations

who's coming who's going — we walk to the gate

trying to guess

"is it raining?"

not raining

noontime stagnates the monotony

the stink of the shitcan

the newspaper gnawing at

the long day: the usual news

Qui

carnevale d'esilio

e bestemmie — fuori

di mortaretti

        'che maschera sono'

        non sono eguale

        'che maschera porto'

        sono eguale

cristo impostore, riconoscimi

esercita pietà

sono il dannato

Here
a carnival of exiles
and curses — outside
the fireworks
        "which mask is me"
        I'm not that
        "which mask am I wearing"
        that's what I am
impostor christ, acknowledge me
practice compassion
I am the damned

Il cubicolo è un forno che trasuda

l'umore di me alle prese con la forza

e l'atto di scontare un vivere

ingombro di spurgo

    — cosa serve aggiustare

il perché delle menzogne

l'immensità della pena più grande

di me in questi dintorni

se oltre l'incubo

non so altra percezione

The cell is an oven that sweats out

my spirit grappling with their power

and the act of atoning for a life

choked with trash

　　　　　— what's the good of adjusting

to the why of their lies

the immense pain larger than I

in this scenario

if beyond the nightmare

I find no other knowledge

Arso dalle azioni di chiunque

annoto i crimini —

                     pure qui la vita

disfa la vita   fruga

interpreta le ragioni   forma e scombina

codici irrazionali

e benché annusi una ricordanza d'uomo

nelle piaghe ripugnanti e menti

carbonizzate dall'odio

non concepisco un lazzaro o un cristo

deforme

Consumed by the actions of — whoever —

I take notes on crimes —

here also life

demolishes life   roots out

motives construes them   makes/breaks

meaningless codes

and though I sniff intimations of man

in loathsome body sores and minds

scorched black by hate

I can't imagine a lazarus or a tainted

christ

Importunato dalle pazienze   i dubbi

l'ambiguità

mi guasta le cellule il vostro microbo

di pace finta — questa larva dilegua

se dissento

se vulnerabile all'insidia biascico

parole vere

se rumino l'attesa di chi

                        di che

                        di me stesso

Patience importunes me / doubts

ambiguity

my cells infected with your virus of feigned

peace — this phantom vanishes

if dissenting I say no

if vulnerable to the snare I mumble

true words

if I ponder in longing for whom

for what

for my own self

La palma lingueggia

lingueggia la pioggia lustrando i crani

semi della prossima sventura

che in agguato già lingueggia prostituta

The palm tree wags its tongues

the rain lashes its tongues polishing skulls

seeds of the next misfortune

a whore in ambush already licking her tongue

Poter combaciare la notte con la palma

che alza un sapore verde

ma il tarlo d'uomo rode

'non c'è angolo dove nascondersi'

al mio intrico si intìma

una lunga indifesa

un maturare incerto

           — solo c'è luogo

nel cranio di Villon

e sotto la palma che a lingue corrosive

spula la luce demente di Nerval

nello sguardo narcotico

If I could blend the night with the palm tree

breathing a green savor

but the human termite gnaws at me

"there's no place to hide"

into my tangle insinuates

a long defenselessness

a doubtful ripening

               — there's only space

in Villon's skull

and under the palm whose caustic tongues

fan the mad light of Nerval

into my drugged stare.

Dalla palma nel cortile la civetta stride

per il topo che sono — un fetore

di bugliolo m'incrosta la gola

e l'impeto della notte

mi spacca la mente

    (mi scaglio nel breve passato

    mi tolgo le scarpe

    ai fossi strappo le canne per soffiarvi

    una bolla di mondo . . .

    e sogno splendidi anarchici)

An owl in the jailyard palm
hoots for the mouse I am — the shit
bucket bites my gullet
and the plunge of night
unhinges my mind

       (I rush at my brief past
       pull these boots off
       yank reeds out of ditches for blowing
       the world like a bubble . . .
       and I dream of magnificent anarchists)

Anch'io incrudelito dall'usanza

da studi sulla rana sul granchio

scosciati vivi

al tavolo della scienza sviscero

ogni forma di vita per concepire quello

che ci definisce: arma   sangue —

imito il dio del verbo

onoro la sua opera

So I grow cruel through habit

studying the frog the crab

legs torn off alive

on the scienceroom table I gut

life in every form to conceive just

what defines us: weapons   blood —

I copy god which is the word

I honor his work

La nudezza dei pozzi mi secca

il corpo fisso alla branda

e assopisco nelle mie forti

braccia umane

The nakedness of the wells saps

my body fixed to the cot

and I doze off in my own strong

human arms

Aggiusto lo sguardo   riconto gli anni

anni igannati pentiti regalati

alla famelica babilonia

se il domani fosse certo potrei forse

sostenere il morso

in me che segregato non indovino quale

luce mi darà vigore —

                        intanto in questo cubicolo

mi mangio maturando e sulla pietra

raspo per una vita dissimile

I adjust my glance   I count the years
years cheated regretted gifted
to ravenous Babylon

if tomorrow were only sure I could perhaps
survive the deep bites inside me
isolated — unable to guess what light
will give me strength —
                        meanwhile in this cubicle
coming of age I gnaw at myself
and scrape on stone for a different life

Una scatola

batteriologica un tubo di provini

chimici e da qui si comincia il nuovo:

uomo ovoidale

tutto testa calva

e privo delle decadenze

che si conosce dai testi di storia

si cominci — ogni azione ogni cosa

andrà per il meglio se arriveremo in tempo

a non interromperci di scatto

con qualcosa che . . .

A bacteriological
kit a chemistry test tube
from here we could start again:

ovoid man
head all over bald
devoid of those corruptions
well known in history texts

again it begins — every action every
thing will be for the best if we arrive in time
without the sudden interruption of
whatever that...

Anni verdi rivengono

ora che pesano le pietre / ogni anno

una pietra nel mare sottostante e non so

ch'io sia — a bracciate mi spiego

io maldestro nuotatore

      (erano bianche le strade

         andavo per sentieri allagati da orti

         liquidi di sole e contro i pali

         del telegrafo sibilava la fionda)

ma un pugno stupendo di nocche mi resta

ora che anni di granito pesano

e alla forza rozza che ha odio soccombo

pelle   mente   verbo

The green years come back
now that these stones weigh me down / each season
a stone in the sea and I don't know
who I am — trying myself with wild
strokes, a bad swimmer

        (once the roads were dust-white
           I wandered along ways flooded with gardens
           fluid with sun and my slingshot
           would hiss against the telegraph poles)

but still I keep a marvelous fist of knuckles
now that the granite years hang heavy
and I succumb to the rough rages of hate
flesh   mind   word

La tarda lingua della viltà e precauzione

non impedisce alla mia età ostile

di rivedere l'Adige

e di mozzare il guaire di tutti

totale insulto

con i denti aguzzi che schizzano veleno

qui e dove non ho altro da dire che

Ce monde n'est qu'abusion

Tongues of cowardice and caution come too late
to stop me in my adverse time
from seeing the Adige again
and cutting short your yelps
— you the total insult —
with my sharp teeth that squirt poison
here and where I have nothing else to say but
Ce monde n'est qu'abusion

IV. IL MURO LUSTRO D'ARIA

IV. THE SHINING WALL OF AIR

C'è in me dello spazio
usurpabile — cerchio
o cono che sia . . .

solo so che nella vertigine
il ragnatelo blocca l'incertezza

There's in me that usurpable
space — circle
or cone or whatever . . .

only this I know in my vertigo
the spider's web blocks the vagaries

Il fiore selvaggio delle tenebre

mi scotta sulla fronte

e mentre indietreggia ed impiccolisce

e dilegua

ingoio rospi / questi omuncoli da circo —

è ora di rinunciare il fuoco per le tenebre

The savage flower of the dark

sears my forehead

and while it draws back and gets smaller

vanishing

I gulp toads / mindless homunculi —

it was time to forsake the fire for darkness

Una mosca adolescente bruisce
sulla gamella calda di zuppa
annunziando l'infezione
e gira l'orlo come sulle labbra
di me che sogno di uccidermi

A young fly bustles
over the bowl of hot soup
announcing contagion
and rides the rim as around my lips
while I'm dreaming of suicide

Si decentra la notte sul muro si decentra

michelangiolesca

la lesione dell'occhio

la cella costringe silenzio

si spacca il silenzio alle sbarre e il trauma

è combustione

— io

groviglio di piedi e mani

prevenendomi

farnetico perfezione

urlo al muro il muro

assorbe   da me l'eco risponde

alla sagoma straniera

Night's off kilter on the wall, off center
the michelangelesque
lesion of the eye

the cell compels silence
shattering silence at the bars and trauma
is fuel

        — I
        a tangle of hands and feet
        forestalling myself
        rave perfection

I howl at the wall the wall
sucks it in   out of me echo answers
to my shape, a stranger

Nella desertica vastità delle acque

non un segno

d'arrivo per gli occhi increduli costanti

a un miraggio di scoglio

e agonizzo alla gola per la conquista

dell'impossibile elemento

che mi possiede

In the desert vastness of waters

no sign

of arrival for the eye unbelieving pursuing

a mirage of rock

and my gullet's in agony to vanquish

the improbable element

possessing me

Preciso il polso ha scoppi d'ali —
qualcuno raccoglie lo sguardo su me
che voglio involarmi ma non tento
la paura del vuoto

resto
piedi sudici di terra
afferrato al muro

lo sguardo si diparte e vendicativa
una risata mi regola il polso

The pulse is punctual, now breaks into wings —
someone narrows his look at me
who am hot to take off but don't tempt
the terror of the void

                I stop
                feet dirty as earth
                hands hung at the wall

the stare turns back and a vengeful
laugh corrects my pulse

Ti somiglio nel balzo nel belato

e neanch'io ho protesta

o protezione

      — il coltello

che brutalmente ti affascina

alla carotide mi è uno sfregio

permanente

I am like you in your leaping your bleating

and I too have no right of protest

or protection

　　　　— the knife

that brutally dazzles you

leaves your permanent gash

at my throat

Ti si offende — si insiste a dire
che t'ingrassi nello sterco
ma io so qual'è
la verità: segui l'obbligo della
condizione
        — tolto dal trogolo
corda al muso oblungo non hai diritto,
resiste l'intuizione quella consapevolezza
ma sei rattenuto
malmenato sulla cassa rovesciata
        e ti si sgozza l'intelligenza
mentre il sangue ti sballotta
e mi sballotta in rantolo

How we insult you, insist
you fatten on filth
but I know
what the truth is: follow the conditions that
fate forced on you
                — dragged here from the trough
a rope around your blunt snout, you have no say
— intuition resists, that deep knowledge
but you're held down
tortured on the upturned crate
                your intelligence slaughtered
as the blood whirls you about
whirls me with a death rattle

Io
albero che scrolla secchezza
so quale vampa isterilisce il corpo

groviglio di radici farnetico
al muro lustro d'aria
e prevenendosi
la morte medita perfezione

ecco il vento
prendermi sotto — cenere
semina il suolo con il finale
no / no / no

I

am this tree shrugging its dry hide

knowing just what blaze barrens the flesh

am a knot of delirious roots

at the shining wall of air

anticipating

death that plots perfection

here is the wind

taking me under — ashes

sow the earth with my final

no / no / no

Biographical notes

Alfredo de Palchi — born in 1926, raised fatherless by an anarchist grandfather in the province of Verona, Italy. Develops lifelong interests in art, literature and music.

World War II, tortured by Fascists. After the war, refuses military draft, arrested by the Communist Partisans. From 1945 to 1951, political prisoner. Scratches first poem on a cell wall in Naples in 1946. Begins serious writing in 1947, when encouraged by an older poet. From 1947 to 1951, completes two collections of poetry. The first accepted for publication by a well-known literary critic, then lost. The second: *The Scorpion's Dark Dance*.

Fall of 1951, continues to defy Italian army. Officer in charge considers him incorrigible and releases him as unstable. Leaves Italy for Paris. With Paris as home base, travels through Europe, spends time in Barcelona, Spain. In 1956, departs for New York. Arrives on Columbus day.

Early years in New York, supports self with menial jobs, becomes active in poetry circles. Helps to translate major modern Italian poets, including Eugenio Montale. In 1961, helps to organize a reading of Montale at the 92nd Street YMCA, in cooperation with Robert Lowell. Since 1960, Associate Editor of *Chelsea*, a literary magazine published in New York.

During the sixties works as American correspondent for the weekly literary journal *La Fiera Letteraria* and Radio-TV of Lugano, Switzerland.

In 1966, assigned with Sonia Raiziss to the Italian section of the six-language anthology, *Modern European Poetry*, published by Bantam Books. Their translations introduce modern Italian poets to American readers.

In 1967, publishes first book, *Sessioni con l'analista* (Arnoldo Mondadori Editore: Milan). Translated by I.L. Salomon as *Sessions with My Analyst* (October House: New York/London), 1970. Receives positive reviews.

From 1967 to 1987, completes three more collections of poetry. In 1988, publishes second book, *Mutazioni* (Campanotto Editore: Udine). Book wins national literary prize.

Since 1970, sells Italian art books to libraries such as The Frick Art Reference Library, The Pierpont Morgan Library and The National Gallery.

Presently preparing collections of poetry and prose for publication.

Works by Alfredo de Palchi

Translations of modern Italian poets in the *Atlantic Monthly* (1958), *The Quarterly Review of Literature, Poetry* and *Eugenio Montale: Selected Poems* (New Directions).

Co-editor, Italian section of *Modern European Poetry* (Bantam Books, 1966).

Sessioni con l'analista (Arnoldo Mondadori Editore: Milan, 1967).

Sessions with My Analyst (October House: New York/London, 1970). Available in paperback and hardcover, October House, Box 454, Stonington, Connecticut 06378.

Mutazioni (Campanotto Editore: Udine, 1988).

Works by Sonia Raiziss

La poésie américaine "moderniste" 1910-1940 (Mercure de France: Paris, 1948).

The Metaphysical Passion: Seven Modern Poets and the Seventeenth-Century Tradition (University of Pennsylvania Press, 1952; reprinted by Greenwood Press: Westport, Conn., 1970).

Editor, Italian section of *Modern European Poetry* (Bantam Books, 1966).

Bucks County Blues (New Rivers Press, 1977).

Of related interest...

DE PALCHI, Alfredo. *Sessions with My Analyst.* tr. by I. L. Salomon. 192p. October House. 1971.

Confessional poetry by an Italian now living in the United States, this work is more polished and less self-indulgent than its American counterparts. De Palchi writes of the fearsome, pitiless world of post-World War II Italy, and of later refinements of cruelty he found in New York and — more terrifyingly — within himself. The final section becomes more elliptical and fragmented as the poet struggles to speak, to communicate, in an increasingly incoherent world. Not for the fainthearted, this is a powerful and original volume of poems. Salomon's translations are amazingly good, and the publisher deserves praise for this bilingual edition. — Priscilla Whitmore, *Library Journal*, September 15, 1971.